The Wright Brothers

A Flying Start

written by Elizabeth MacLeod

Kids Can Press

For darling Jordie and his beloved Opa, dearly loved and greatly missed.

Consultants

Dawne Dewey, Head, Special Collections and Archives, Wright State University

Peter Jakab, Curator, Aeronautics Division, National Air and Space Museum, Smithsonian Institution

Acknowledgments

It is such a pleasure to work again with the patient, dedicated and fabulous team of Patricia Buckley, photo researcher; Karen Powers, designer; and especially Val Wyatt, editor. Many thanks to you all for working so hard on this book and for making it take flight!

I also really appreciate all the time that the Kids Can Press Technical Services department put into this book — thank you so much Rachel Di Salle, Sherill Chapman, Katie Collett and Andrew Metcalfe. Thanks to the entire Kids Can Press team, especially Rivka Cranley and Valerie Hussey.

I'm extremely grateful to Dawne Dewey and Peter Jakab for their interest in this book and all the time they graciously spent reviewing the pages so carefully.

Many thanks to Robert Bishop, Bill and Riek Brouwer, Laurie Dullart and Brian Everett.

And love always to Paul for flying me to the moon.

Text © 2002 Elizabeth MacLeod
Illustrations of Orville and Wilbur Wright © 2002 Barbara Spurll

All rights reserved. No part of this publication may be reproduced, stored in a retrieval system or transmitted, in any form or by any means, without the prior written permission of Kids Can Press Ltd. or, in case of photocopying or other reprographic copying, a license from CANCOPY (Canadian Copyright Licensing Agency), 1 Yonge Street, Suite 1900, Toronto, ON, M5E 1E5.

Kids Can Press acknowledges the financial support of the Ontario Arts Council, the Canada Council for the Arts and the Government of Canada, through the BPIDP, for our publishing activity.

Published in Canada by
Kids Can Press Ltd.
29 Birch Avenue
Toronto, ON M4V 1E2

Published in the U.S. by
Kids Can Press Ltd.
2250 Military Road
Tonawanda, NY 14150

www.kidscanpress.com

Edited by Valerie Wyatt
Designed by Karen Powers

Printed in Hong Kong by Wing King Tong Company Limited

The hardcover edition of this book is smyth sewn casebound.
The paperback edition of this book is limp sewn with a drawn-on cover.

CM 02 0 9 8 7 6 5 4 3 2 1
CM PA 02 0 9 8 7 6 5 4 3 2 1

National Library of Canada Cataloguing in Publication Data

MacLeod, Elizabeth
   The Wright brothers : a flying start

Includes index.

ISBN 1-55074-933-1 (bound)   ISBN 1-55074-935-8 (pbk.)

1. Wright, Orville, 1871–1948 — Juvenile literature. 2. Wright, Wilbur, 1867–1912 — Juvenile literature. 3. Aeronautics — United States — Biography — Juvenile literature. I. Title.

TL540.W7M32 2002   j629.13'0092'273   C2001-901519-4

Photo credits

Every reasonable effort has been made to trace ownership of and give accurate credit to copyrighted material. Information that would enable the publisher to correct any discrepancies in future editions would be appreciated.

Abbreviations

t = top; b = bottom; c = center; l = left; r = right

Frank Baldasserra: 12 (b). **Bettmann/Corbis/Magma:** 11 (t). **EyeWire:** front cover (t) and 13 (t). **Collection of Henry Ford Museum and Greenfield Village:** 3 (bl), 9 (tr, c). **Library of Congress:** front cover (c), 1, 4 (b), 5 (t), 12 (t, c), 15 (t, c), 17 (all), 18, 19 (all), 20, 21 (t, cl), 23 (tl, c), 26 (b), 31 (cl), back cover (bl, cl, br). **NASA:** 4 (bl), 28 (t, c, b), 29 (b), 31 (b), back cover (tr). **National Air and Space Museum, Smithsonian Institution:** 3 (cl [SI-A-43323]), 7 (tl [SI-A-19627]), 10 (SI-A-29311-K), 11 (c [SI-A-48093]), (b [SI-A-16539-A]), 13 (b [SI-A-43323]), 16 (SI-A-2708-G), 25 (b [SI-A-52382]), 31 (t [SI-A-48093-Fl]), back cover (tl [SI-A-29311-K]). **U.S. National Archives:** (c [NW-DNS-80-G-418418]). **U.S. National Parks Service:** p. 4 (t). **Wright State University:** front cover (b), 3 (t, cr), 5 (b), 6 (t, b), 7 (tc, tr, b), 8, 9 (tl, b), 14, 15 (b), 21 (b), 22, 23 (tr, b), 24 (t,b), 25 (t, c), 26 (t), 27 (t, b), 29 (t), 31 (cr).

The sketch on pages 3 and 21 and on the back cover (tc) is from an illustration by James MacDonald in *How We Invented the Airplane: An Illustrated History* by Fred C. Kelly, published by Dover Publications, © 1953 by Fred C. Kelly, new material © 1988 by Dover Publications.

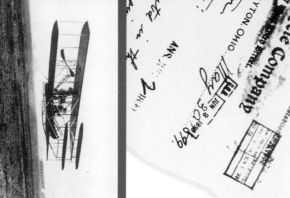

Contents

CRADLE

LEFT

Meet the Wright brothers

About 100 years ago, in just 12 seconds, the world changed forever. On December 17, 1903, near Kitty Hawk, North Carolina, Wilbur and Orville Wright made the first controlled, powered flight. The Wrights' airplane, or flying machine as it was called then, traveled only 36 m (120 ft.) — a little more than half the length of a pro-hockey rink — but the brothers had achieved something that no one else had.

Although no one knew it at the time, their flight would completely change the way we live. Thanks to the Wright brothers, people can now cross the Atlantic Ocean in hours instead of days. Parcels move across North America overnight. And astronauts have even made it to the moon.

The Wright brothers — their family and close friends called them Will and Orv — never got more than a high school education and were self-taught engineers. They had no special technical training, but they were keen observers and kept excellent records of their experiments. The brothers were shy men, but Wilbur had a strong drive to succeed, and Orville had a natural talent for inventing.

What made these inventors dream of flying?

"At the time we first flew our power plane we were not thinking of any practical uses at all. We just wanted to show that it was possible to fly."

— Orville

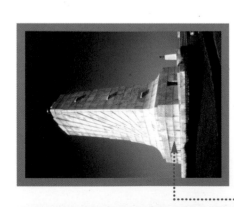

The inscription on the Wright Brothers National Memorial near Kitty Hawk, North Carolina, reads: "In commemoration of the conquest of the air by the brothers Wilbur and Orville Wright. Conceived by genius. Achieved by dauntless resolution and unconquerable faith."

The Lockheed SR-71 Blackbird is one of the world's fastest airplanes, flying faster than 3540 km/h (2200 m.p.h.). See how different it looks from the Wrights' first flying machine?

Before building their first powered flying machine, the brothers experimented with gliders. Here Wilbur test-flies an early glider.

Wilbur and Orville weren't twins but they thought alike. As they worked together on their flying machines, they might suddenly start whistling or singing the same song.

Early years

Wilbur and Orville raced to the door. Their father was home from a trip, and he usually brought them a present! Milton Wright was barely through the door when he tossed something into the air. It flew across the room as the brothers raced after it.

It was a Pénaud helicopter, a toy that looked like a miniature helicopter. The boys were fascinated by it. When the toy broke, they repaired it and even built their own versions. Wilbur and Orville tried to make larger and larger models and couldn't figure out why they wouldn't fly.

Building and repairing came easily to the brothers. With five kids in the family, there wasn't a lot of money for new toys, so they had to make their own. The children were named Reuchlin (the oldest), then Lorin, Wilbur, Orville, and their only sister, Katharine. Their father thought Wright was such an ordinary name that his children needed distinctive first names.

As kids, Wilbur and Orville loved fixing machines and experimenting. To earn extra money, they sold kites to the neighborhood children. Orville tried other money-making schemes, such as collecting bones for a fertilizer plant, gathering old wood and metal for a junkyard and even putting on a circus.

The brothers were also interested in printing. When Wilbur was in his teens, he invented a machine to fold papers for mailing. Orville was about 14 when he and a friend set up a small printing firm. To get more experience, Orville worked for a printer for two summers. Then, with Wilbur's help, he built another printing press, using a gravestone for part of it, and opened his own print shop.

Sometimes the brothers' experiments and hobbies got in the way of school. They skipped classes, and once Orville was even expelled.

At 18, Wilbur planned to go to Yale University and become a minister. But one day, while playing hockey, a teammate accidentally hit him and knocked out his front teeth. Surgery and false teeth restored Wilbur's face, but he lost his confidence. During his long recovery, Wilbur gave up the idea of university. Besides, Orville wanted to start a newspaper and would need Wilbur's help.

Wilbur and Orville's father, Milton, was a minister with the Church of the United Brethren in Christ and later became a bishop. Their mother, Susan, could build or fix almost anything — skills the brothers inherited.

The brothers called their Pénaud helicopter "The Bat." It was made of cork, bamboo and paper and was powered by a rubber band.

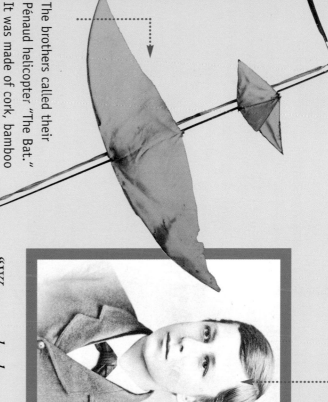

"We were lucky enough to grow up in a home environment where there was always much encouragement to children to pursue intellectual interests; to investigate whatever aroused curiosity." — Orville

Wilbur was four years older than Orville. Here's Wilbur at 12 (left) and Orville at 8 (right).

I was born in Millville, Indiana, in 1867, and Orville was born in Dayton, Ohio, in 1871.

MICHIGAN

INDIANA

Millville

Dayton

Columbus ★

OHIO

Lake Erie

KENTUCKY

WEST VIRGINIA

PENNSYLVANIA

The Wrights lived in this house in Dayton, Ohio, for 42 years. They also lived in Iowa and Indiana.

Newspapers and bicycles

Orville's dream of publishing a newspaper came true on March 1, 1889, with Wilbur's help. Wilbur edited the *West Side News*, a weekly paper, while Orville printed and sold it. With the two brothers working together, the paper did so well that after a year they decided to give it a new name and publish it every day. But the new *Evening Item* couldn't compete with other daily papers, and the last issue appeared just four months later.

The print shop was doing well, but the brothers wanted a new challenge. What to do next? Cycling was a growing sport, and Orville often competed in local races. (Wilbur preferred long rides in the country.) Friends were always asking the Wrights to repair their bicycles. So when they were in their early twenties, the brothers opened a bicycle shop called the Wright Cycle Company. They weren't alone. More and more stores opened, and competition got tougher and tougher.

Business was slow. Wilbur thought again about going to college — he'd read and studied a lot while recovering from his accident, and his amazing memory retained most of what he read. But Orville convinced him to stay to help expand the bicycle business. Instead of just selling and repairing bicycles, they would also build them. That was just the kind of challenge Wilbur and Orville loved.

As they worked around the shop, the brothers were often visited by their nephews and nieces. Wilbur and Orville would take time to make toys, play games or cook delicious fudge. After hours, they worked hard on the family home, adding porches and building a fireplace. If the brothers couldn't find a tool they needed, they made their own. They were keen photographers, too, and had a dark room for developing photos.

Then in August 1896, Orville suddenly became ill with typhoid fever, a severe illness caused by bacteria. For weeks he lay unconscious, close to death. Wilbur stayed with him, nursing him and reading to him. Finally, in October, Orville's fever broke and he began to get better.

Wilbur read a lot during those long hours by Orville's bed, including an article about an inventor and his flying machines. Life would never be the same for the Wright brothers.

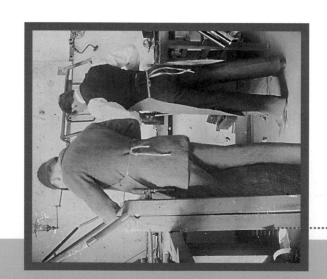

Orville (right) and the brothers' assistant, Ed Sines, in the bicycle shop in 1897. Orville and Ed had been friends since they were kids.

Wilbur and I once made a huge bicycle-built-for-two from spare parts in our shop.

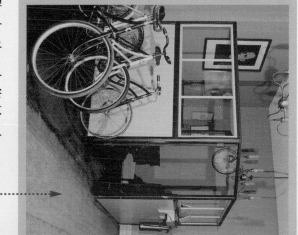

Here is the Wrights' bicycle shop. Their next-door neighbor was an undertaker.

The brothers built bicycles on the second floor of the shop and sold bikes and parts on the first floor.

Early bicycles had huge front wheels, tiny back wheels and were difficult to ride. But the new bicycles that the Wright brothers sold had two wheels of the same size, like today's bicycles. They were called safety bicycles because they were so much easier to ride.

The first issue of the *West Side News* was published on March 1, 1889. Paul Laurence Dunbar, a friend of Orville's, often wrote for the paper. Dunbar would later become the first nationally famous African-American poet.

9

Up in the air

The inventor of flying machines whom Wilbur had read about was Otto Lilienthal. He was a German engineer, famous for his experiments with gliders. But Lilienthal wasn't the first to try to invent a flying machine.

Back in 1500, inventor and artist Leonardo da Vinci sketched airplane-like machines, although he never built them. Then, in 1783, Joseph and Étienne Montgolfier launched the first hot-air balloon in France. No one knew if it was safe to breathe so far above Earth. To find out, the brothers tied a basket to the balloon and placed a duck, a rooster and a sheep in it. All three animals survived — although the sheep stepped on the rooster. A few weeks later, two men went up in the balloon. But balloonists could only drift with the wind. What inventors wanted was a machine whose flight could be *controlled*.

All serious inventors knew the work of Daniel Bernoulli, a Swiss scientist. In 1738 he realized that the faster a fluid, such as air, moves, the less pressure it exerts. This is called "Bernoulli's principle," the basis for all flight. For example, a bird's wing is more curved on the top than on the bottom. The air going *over* the wing has to go a little farther than the air going *under* the wing because of that curve. But it has to do it in the same amount of time, so it has to go *faster*, too.

Bernoulli discovered that the faster the air moves, the less pressure it exerts. So the air under the wing pushes up harder than the air on top pushes down. This extra pressure pushes — or lifts — the bird into the air.

British experimenter Sir George Cayley designed several gliders, using Bernoulli's principle. In 1849 he launched a glider that carried a 10-year-old boy a short distance. Five years later Cayley sent up his carriage driver in a glider — the driver quit when he landed. But Cayley kept working to build a steerable glider.

Cayley's work inspired Otto Lilienthal. By 1896 Lilienthal had made about 2000 glider flights. His next step was to add power. That's what Lilienthal was doing when his glider crashed and he was killed. His death might have scared off most people, but it didn't frighten the Wright brothers. They were ready to tackle the challenge of flight.

The Montgolfier brothers sent this balloon aloft in 1783.

Orville and I read about other inventors and studied how birds fly.

Some of the flying machines sketched by inventors look so odd that it's hard to believe anyone really thought they could ever fly.

Otto Lilienthal based his work on what he'd learned from watching birds. He was the first to pilot a glider successfully and went on to build 16 different types.

In 1849 Sir George Cayley built the first glider that could carry a person.

According to Bernoulli's principle, the air going over the curved wing of a bird or airplane goes *farther — and faster —* than the air going *under* the wing. The faster-moving air exerts less pressure. So the air under the wing pushes up harder than the air on top pushes down, lifting the bird or airplane into the air.

Don't these machines look strange? Wilbur's and my ideas probably seemed just as weird.

The Wright way

Wilbur and Orville really caught the flying bug when they read about Otto Lilienthal's gliders in the mid-1890s. The Wrights researched flight at their local library, then wrote to the Smithsonian Instituion for a list of books on flight.

Like many other inventors at the time, the Wright brothers wanted to invent a machine capable of powered, controlled flight. They soon realized that such a machine would need three things:

1. Wings strong enough to lift a person into the air.

2. An engine that could move the machine forward fast enough so that air flowing over the wings kept the machine airborne.

3. A way to control its path and direction.

Wilbur and Orville worried most about controlling the flying machine — it was lack of control that had killed Lilienthal. One day, while watching pigeons fly by, Wilbur noticed that one of the birds changed the position of its wing tips to turn. If the brothers could figure out how to change, or "warp," the shape of a machine's wings during flight, they could control its direction.

A little later in the bicycle shop, after fixing a puncture in an inner tube, Wilbur fiddled with the long, narrow cardboard box the inner tube had come in. He twisted the two ends of the box in different directions. When he twisted one way, the top left end of the box and the bottom right were up. When he twisted the other way, the top right and bottom left ends came up. Just like the right and left wings of a bird, he thought. Maybe this was the way to change a flying machine's wings and control flight.

Wilbur and Orville decided to try it. By the summer of 1899, they had built their first model — a double-decker kite — and were ready to test it.

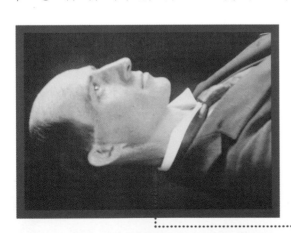

Wilbur (above) was in his late 20s and Orville in his mid 20s when they began researching flight.

"I got more thrill out of flying before I had ever been in the air at all — while lying in bed thinking how exciting it would be to fly."
— Orville

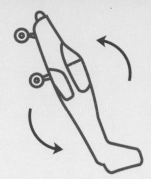

See how a bird can twist or warp its wings to help it turn?

There are three basic movements an airplane can make:

It can **pitch**, which means its nose goes up and down.

It can **roll**, or dip its wings from side to side.

Or it can **yaw** — turn from side to side.

Wilbur wrote to the Smithsonian Institution on his company's letterhead, which featured forget-me-nots and rays of sunshine peeping through clouds.

> In my letter to the Smithsonian, I sketched out our observations about birds' flight.

The Smithsonian Institution;
Washington.

Dear Sirs:

I have been interested in the problem of human flight ever since as a boy...

Go fly a kite!

The double-decker kite that Wilbur and Orville built was equipped with cords attached to its wing tips so the brothers could experiment with wing warping. Pulling the cords twisted the end of the kite's wings. The wing tip that was twisted up would be pushed down by the air rushing past it, and the kite would roll to that side and turn. A similar system using movable controls, such as rudders and ailerons, is used in today's airplanes.

In the spring of 1900, the Wright brothers began building a glider strong enough to carry a person. With such a heavy load, they knew they'd need high winds to launch it. So they wrote to the National Weather Bureau to find the windiest places in the United States. The brothers also contacted flying-machine inventor Octave Chanute, who recommended sand hills for soft landings. Kitty Hawk, North Carolina, fit the bill — it was windy, with lots of sand dunes nearby.

The Wrights set up a tent on the sand. At first, the winds were so strong that it was too dangerous to test their glider. Instead they attached a rope to it and flew it like a kite to learn how it moved. One night the wind buried the glider in the sand. Another time the wind picked up the glider, then smashed it down. But the brothers merely repaired the glider and kept trying.

Finally the weather conditions were just right. On October 3, 1900, with the help of a local man, Bill Tate, the Wrights carried the glider to the highest sand dunes on the island. The area had a threatening name — Kill Devil Hills — but it was the perfect launching point.

Wilbur couldn't resist trying out the glider. With Orville and Tate each holding a wing, and Wilbur in the middle, they ran with the machine into the wind until it began to lift. Then Wilbur scrambled in. But just as the glider lifted him off the ground, he yelled, "Let me down!" Orville yanked the glider down and angrily demanded an explanation. "I promised Pop I'd take care of myself," said his brother.

The brothers flew the glider a few more times before heading home to Dayton on October 23. When they analyzed the glider's flight, they were puzzled. According to Lilienthal's data, it shouldn't have flown the way it did. Wilbur and Orville decided they were incorrect and obviously needed more experience. They would later find out that they were right, and Lilienthal was wrong.

Octave Chanute, a well-known French engineer, had long been interested in flight. Wilbur and Orville read about his work and became friends with him.

Some nights at Kitty Hawk were so cold that Wilbur and I wore our coats, shoes and hats to bed.

Some people think Kitty Hawk is the English pronunciation of the area's Native name, *Chickahauk*, which means "goose hunting grounds." Kill Devil Hills are probably named for a brand of rum found washed ashore many years ago.

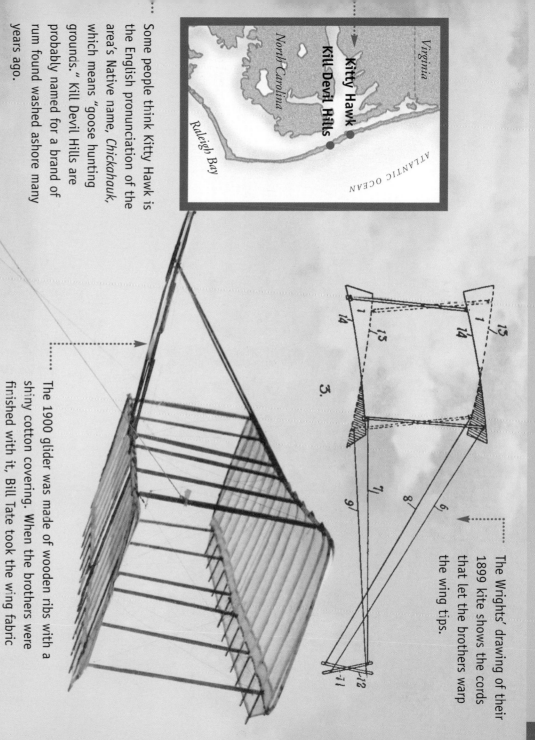

The 1900 glider was made of wooden ribs with a shiny cotton covering. When the brothers were finished with it, Bill Tate took the wing fabric home, and his wife made dresses for their daughters.

The Wrights' drawing of their 1899 kite shows the cords that let the brothers warp the wing tips.

The Wright brothers camped on the sand at Kitty Hawk. Water was in short supply so Wilbur scoured pots and pans with sand.

"The wind shaking the roof and sides of the tent sounds exactly like thunder. When we crawl out of the tent to fix things outside the sand fairly blinds us . . . We came down here for wind and sand, and we have got them."

— Orville

The Wrights go wrong

By the summer of 1901, Wilbur and Orville were ready to return to Kill Devil Hills. They'd built a bigger glider, and Octave Chanute had sent two people he'd worked with to help. But everything went wrong; rain poured down, the brothers were sick, mosquitoes buzzed constantly and one of Chanute's men was useless.

On top of all this, the Wrights' new glider didn't fly very well. Once, with Wilbur aboard, it rose into the air, then almost stopped moving — the same situation that had killed Lilienthal. Luckily, Wilbur was able to land safely. The brothers realized they still had a lot to learn.

A depressed Wilbur and Orville headed home in mid-August. But Chanute reminded them that they had broken all gliding records and knew more than anyone about flying. To take their minds off the disappointing summer, Chanute arranged for Wilbur to speak to an important group of engineers in Chicago. (Orville was too shy to make speeches, even after he became famous.)

Wilbur had to borrow Orville's clothes — Orville was always a better dresser — but his speech was clear and well illustrated with charts and slides. The audience was fascinated by the brothers' work, and Wilbur's speech was reprinted around the world.

Back in Dayton, the brothers were filled with doubts. Why should they achieve their goal of powered, controlled flight when so many others, better educated and skilled, had failed? Orville decided to recheck the data they'd collected from other inventors' work. He attached small wings of different shapes to a bicycle wheel tipped on its side and turned it to see how the wings reacted.

Orville soon realized that the data he and Wilbur — and other inventors — had used were wrong, but he didn't know by how much. To find out, he rigged up a wind tunnel in a 46-cm (18-in.) long wooden box. The wind tunnel allowed the Wrights to test how air moves over a wing. It worked well, and Orville spent hours experimenting.

The brothers built a bigger wind tunnel and tested more than 200 wing shapes. Their conclusions were astounding; all the previous data were wrong and the Wrights were right. The brothers finally had the information they needed about wing shape and lift to design a flying machine.

> *The second wind tunnel Orville and I built was 1.8 m (6 ft.) long and had a fan at the end.*

This is a replica of the wind tunnel used by Orville and Wilbur. Their experiments were tedious and slow, but the brothers were making new discoveries.

Fellow inventor Octave Chanute enjoyed visiting Wilbur and Orville. He didn't realize how close the brothers were to reaching their goal.

This picture was taken seconds before the glider, with Wilbur at the controls, stopped flying and almost crashed.

"We doubted that we would ever resume our experiments. At this time I made the prediction that man would sometime fly, but that it would not be in our lifetime."

—Wilbur

You can see how big the 1901 glider is compared to Orville. It was the largest glider ever flown up to this point.

Orville (back to the camera) and Wilbur tried flying their glider as a kite. The "wing" above Orville's head was attached to the front of the glider to balance it as it climbed and descended.

Add some power

By September 1902, the brothers were back at Kill Devil Hills with an even bigger glider. For the first time, they added an immovable, vertical tail. But this one was hard to control, too. One night while lying in bed, Orville figured out that its immovable tail might be the problem. If the tail could move, maybe the pilot could change the glider's position and stabilize it.

Orville knew he'd have to be careful how he suggested this change to Wilbur. As the older brother, Wilbur often seemed to automatically reject Orville's ideas. But Wilbur agreed this time and suggested connecting a tail control to the wing-warping system.

The new movable rudder was a success. It allowed the rudder to turn and to reduce the drag (air resistance) on the glider during wing warping. This was an important breakthrough, and the control system in today's airplanes is based on it.

The brothers went up in their improved glider more than 700 times. The glider could stay airborne for up to 26 seconds and had good lift and control. Finally the Wright brothers felt it was time to add power.

Soon after Wilbur and Orville returned to Dayton in November 1902, they began work in their bicycle shop on a new flying machine. It was so big that when a customer entered the shop, one of the brothers had to scoot out the side door and around to the front to wait on him.

The brothers wrote to motor manufacturers, asking them to build a strong, light engine. Some manufacturers were willing, but no one could do it for the money Wilbur and Orville had. So, as with many other things, the brothers designed an engine themselves.

The Wrights also researched propellers. They investigated ship propellers, but found they were built by trial and error and weren't based on scientific calculations. Once again the brothers had to do their own research. In a few months they had built the two 2.4 m (8 ft.) propellers they needed.

Wilbur and Orville knew that many other inventors were trying to build flying machines. Would someone steal their ideas? They tried to patent the design of their flying machine, but the U.S. Patent Office, tired of seeing "crazy" flying-machine designs, told the Wrights their ideas would never work.

Before Wilbur and Orville began their experiments at Kill Devil Hills in the fall of 1902, they first improved the shed they lived in there. That included building on a kitchen.

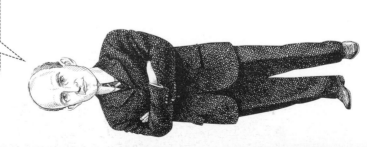

Orville did all the cooking at Kill Devil Hills.

The 1902 glider had a vertical rudder on the back to prevent spins and stalls.

"We had been unable to find anything of value in any of the works to which we had access, so that we worked out a theory of our own on the subject and soon discovered, as we usually do, that all the propellers built heretofore are all wrong."

— Orville

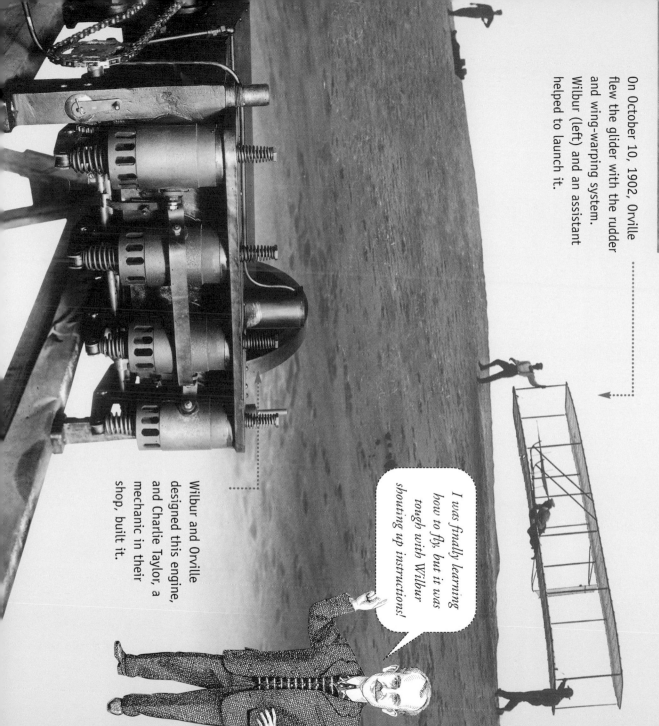

On October 10, 1902, Orville flew the glider with the rudder and wing-warping system. Wilbur (left) and an assistant helped to launch it.

Wilbur and Orville designed this engine, and Charlie Taylor, a mechanic in their shop, built it.

I was finally learning how to fly, but it was tough with Wilbur shouting up instructions!

"They done it!"

"After these years of experience I look with amazement upon our audacity in attempting flights with a new and untried machine under such circumstances."

— Orville

The Wrights left Dayton on September 23, 1903, determined to make at least one powered flight in their new machine. First they practiced in last year's glider. Then they tested the new engine, but ran into the same bad luck that had haunted them the summer before. The engine backfired, the propeller shafts cracked and the weather grew colder.

It wasn't until December 14 that the brothers were ready to attempt powered flight. The winds were light, so the Wrights decided to use gravity to help them get the *Flyer* into the air. They built a long rail up a nearby hill, and, with the help of local lifeguards, rolled the flying machine up the rail on two bicycle-wheel hubs. The *Flyer* would roll down the rail to get enough speed to become airborne.

By mid-afternoon the Wrights were almost ready. They tossed a coin to decide who would climb into the *Flyer*. Wilbur won — was he about to become the first person to fly?

The lifeguards watched anxiously while Orville tried to steady the flying machine as it zoomed down the rail. He let go and it lifted into the air. Then suddenly it dropped and caught a wing in the sand. The *Flyer* had crashed after only three seconds.

Wilbur climbed out, and the brothers inspected the damage. Luckily it wasn't too bad. Two days later, the flying machine was repaired and it was Orville's turn. But the winds weren't strong enough. The Wrights moved the rail to level ground and waited.

The brothers awoke on December 17 to a windy day. But they knew if they didn't try again soon, they might have to wait until spring. Wilbur and Orville signaled the lifeguards: they were ready. The flying machine was on its launching rail, its engine running smoothly.

Orville eased into the *Flyer* and released the anchor — and he was airborne! The flight lasted only 12 seconds, but the Wright brothers had made history with the first powered and controlled flight. One lifeguard ran into town yelling, "They done it! They done it!"

The brothers made four flights, with Wilbur making the longest — 260 m (852 ft.) — and staying airborne for 59 seconds. The Wrights telegraphed their friends and family but told no one else. They wanted to keep their design secret so no one could copy it. But the news leaked out, thanks to the telegraph operators.

Orville assembling the *Flyer* in the hangar at Kill Devil Hills.

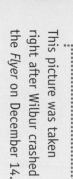

The winds were freezing cold and whipped sand into our eyes. But Orv and I were determined to fly.

This picture was taken right after Wilbur crashed the *Flyer* on December 14.

-- December 17 — Success at last! Wilbur stands by while Orville becomes the first person to fly.

Orville's name is misspelled in this telegram he sent to his father, and the brothers' longest flight was actually 59 seconds.

RECEIVED at

... is a theory of Liars only by repeating a message or a message back to be originating station for comparison, and the company will not hold itself liable for errors or delays in transmission or delivery of UNREPEATED MESSAGES, beyond the amount of tolls paid thereon, nor in any case where the claim is not presented in writing within sixty days after the message is filed with the Company for transmission.
This is an UNREPEATED MESSAGE, and is delivered by request of the sender, under the conditions named above.
ROBERT C. CLOWRY, President and General Manager.

ON TELEGRAPH COMPANY.
INCORPORATED
CABLE SERVICE TO ALL THE WORLD.

IN AMERICA.

176 C KA CS 33 Paid.
Kitty Hawk N C Dec 17
Bishop M Wright   Via Norfolk Va

7 Hawthorne St

Success four flights thursday morning all against twenty one mile wind started from level with engine power alone average speed through air thirty one miles longest 57 seconds inform Press home Christmas .

Orevelle Wright

525p

RIGHT

LEFT

CRADLE

This sketch shows how the wings on the Wrights' airplane could be twisted or warped. If the pilot shifted his hips a little to the left on the cradle, for example, the left wing moved lower than the right one, and the flying machine turned to the left.

Ups and downs

You'd think that newspapers everywhere would have carried the story of the Wrights' flight. But most outsiders who heard about it didn't realize what the brothers had done. Others didn't believe them — after all, so many inventors, with better educations, had failed.

Wilbur and Orville kept experimenting. They no longer needed the high winds and soft dunes of Kill Devil Hills, so they worked at Huffman Prairie, 13 km (8 mi.) from their home in Dayton. By January 1904, the brothers were building *Flyer II*, with a new, larger engine. Wild stories buzzed around about the Wrights' flying machines, so Wilbur and Orville invited reporters to watch *Flyer II*'s trial flights in May. The reporters gathered, but bad weather meant the flying machine flew only 9 m (30 ft.). No one was impressed.

In 1905 the Wrights built *Flyer III*. It had separate controls for the rudder and wing-warping system and in October flew an amazing 39 km (24 mi.). The flying machine could stay in the air for more than half an hour. Finally, a really practical airplane!

Wilbur and Orville decided they'd better keep their new airplane design secret. They would not fly again until they had sold it. That took longer than they hoped — almost three years. They kept busy applying for the patent for the airplane and trying to sell it.

The Wright brothers offered their machine to the U.S. government for army use, but there was no interest. However, the governments of France and England *were* interested. In 1907 Wilbur and Orville traveled to Europe and came close to a sale in France.

The brothers returned home at the end of 1907. But they soon realized they'd have to demonstrate their airplane to make the French sale. So on August 8, 1908, near Le Mans, France, Wilbur amazed the watching crowds, although he was airborne for less than two minutes. He made many more flights, some longer than an hour, because so many people wanted to see the airplane fly.

Stories of Wilbur's flights quickly got back to North America. Finally the U.S. Army became interested in the *Flyer III*. In 1908 Orville made performance trials in Fort Myer, Virginia. The early flights went well, but on September 17, a propeller broke. Orville lost control and crashed, killing his passenger, Lieutenant Thomas Selfridge. Orville broke a leg and several ribs and was in the hospital for weeks.

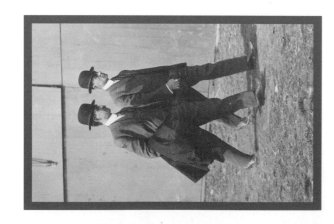

"All question as to who originated the flying machine has disappeared. The furor has been so great as to be troublesome. I cannot even take a bath without having a hundred or two people peeking at me."

— Wilbur

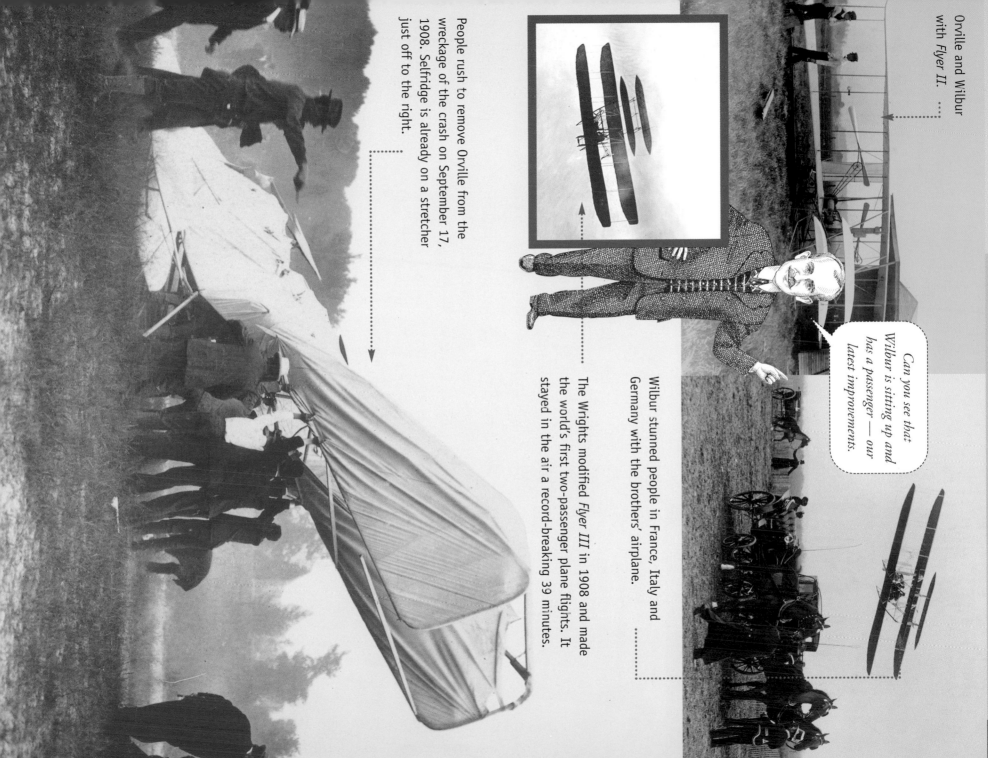

Orville and Wilbur with *Flyer II*.

People rush to remove Orville from the wreckage of the crash on September 17, 1908. Selfridge is already on a stretcher just off to the right.

The Wrights modified *Flyer III* in 1908 and made the world's first two-passenger plane flights. It stayed in the air a record-breaking 39 minutes.

Wilbur stunned people in France, Italy and Germany with the brothers' airplane.

Can you see that Wilbur is sitting up and has a passenger — our latest improvements.

Flying high

When Orville recovered from the Fort Myer crash, he and his sister, Katharine, joined Wilbur in Europe in early 1909. Royalty watched and people cheered as Wilbur shattered flight records for height, time and distance. Orville and Katharine stayed in hotels as they traveled around, but sometimes Wilbur insisted on sleeping in the hangar with the airplane to make sure nothing happened to it.

When the brothers returned to the United States, people finally seemed to understand what they had accomplished. They received a hero's welcome in New York, and their home town of Dayton held a two-day celebration.

More important to the Wright brothers was that their airplanes were selling. In July 1909, the U.S. Army bought the Military Flyer. In November Wilbur and Orville set up the Wright Company in the United States. (Three months earlier they had formed the German-Wright Company to build airplanes in Germany.) Now the brothers were running a factory, testing airplanes and training pilots. They also had to fight lawsuits to protect the patent on their invention.

Wilbur and Orville arranged flying displays to get people interested in airplanes. One year, the Wright Exhibition Company earned over one million dollars from these daredevil exhibitions. But the shows took the brothers away from their research, and as people demanded tougher tricks, pilots were injured or killed. The Wrights later disbanded the flying team.

May 1910 was a month the brothers would always remember. On May 21, Wilbur flew by himself, the last time he would ever pilot an airplane in the United States. A few days later, the Wrights flew together for the first and only time, with Orville at the controls. On May 25, Orville took up their father, who was over 80. As the airplane soared upward, the old man yelled, "Higher, Orville, higher!"

The legal battles the Wright brothers fought wore down Wilbur's health. In early May 1912, he caught typhoid fever. He died on May 30, less than ten years after he and his brother had flown into history.

"Flight was generally looked upon as an impossibility. And scarcely anyone believed in it until he had actually seen it with his own eyes." — Orville

When Katharine, Orville and Wilbur's sister, flew for the first time in France in 1909, Wilbur was at the controls. Notice how Katharine's skirt is tied to keep it from blowing in the wind.

Wilbur amazed millions when he flew up around the Statue of Liberty in 1909. He carried a special canoe to keep the airplane afloat if it went down.

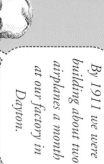

By 1911 we were building about two airplanes a month at our factory in Dayton.

The Wright brothers met King Edward VII of England (on right with beard) in Paris in 1909.

Here's a Model B Flyer being built at the Wright Company factory in Dayton in 1911.

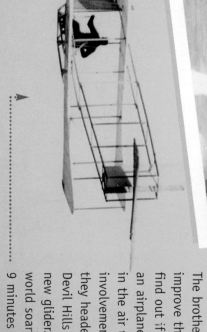

The brothers continued to improve their machines. To find out if they could keep an airplane straight and level in the air without the involvement of the pilot, they headed back to Kill Devil Hills in 1911 with this new glider. Orville set a world soaring record of 9 minutes and 45 seconds.

Final flights

Wilbur's death devastated Orville. His partner of so many years was suddenly gone. Three years later, Orville sold their airplane company. For a short time, he worked as a consulting engineer, but he spent most of his time doing research in his own lab in Dayton.

Orville was greatly saddened by the destruction their invention caused in World Wars I and II. Some people had thought airplanes would bring an end to war. They believed that countries would be afraid to fight each other, since airplanes could carry such deadly weapons and cause so much damage. But the opposite happened. By 1915 the first real fighter airplane appeared, equipped with a machine gun.

When World War I ended in 1918, experienced pilots left the air force and used their skills to dust crops, spot forest fires, do aerial surveying and much more. Airmail service between Washington and New York got off to a rocky start in May 1918 — the first pilot took off in the wrong direction, and the mail had to be sent back by train. Other pilots became "barnstormers." They flew across the country, selling airplane rides and performing stunts, such as walking on the wings of a flying airplane.

For a few years after Wilbur's death, Orville continued to experiment, this time with seaplanes — airplanes with floats so they could take off and land on water. In 1916 he bought an island in Georgian Bay on Lake Huron in Ontario and spent almost every summer there until World War II. Even at that cottage Orville kept inventing. He created machines to ensure a perfect piece of toast every time. He also invented a water-pump system, a rail cart and a clothes washer that used an outboard boat motor. In 1924 Orville applied for his last patent, for a toy clown.

Orville watched the airplane evolve. Passenger airlines formed in the mid-1930s. Airplanes became jet-propelled in 1939, and in 1947, a rocket-powered aircraft flew so fast that it broke the sound barrier.

In October 1947, Orville had a heart attack. It slowed him down a little but he continued working. Then, in 1948, he had a second attack and died three days later, on January 30, 1948. The first person to fly was gone.

Orville climbing into a transport airplane in 1942. The airplane's engines were made by Wright Aeronautical.

Orville took this photo of his St. Bernard, Scipio.

"I don't have any regrets about my part in the invention of the airplane, though no one could deplore more than I do the destruction it has caused."

— Orville

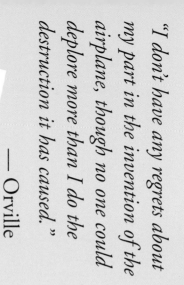

These World War II U.S. Navy warplanes could fly in perfect formation and were deadly bombers.

Orville lived at Hawthorn Hill in Dayton from 1913 to 1948.

I named the mansion "Hawthorn Hill" after the street where my family had lived for so long.

The Dayton-Wright Company was formed in 1917.

"DAYTON-WRIGHT" AIRPLANES

Commercial and Pleasure Aircraft of Distinction

The General Motors Corporation, Dayton-Wright Division, Dayton, Ohio, U.S.A.
"THE BIRTHPLACE OF AVIATION"

Members of the Manufacturers Aircraft Association.

The sky's the limit

A little more than 50 years after the Wright brothers' amazing first flight, engineers launched a satellite into orbit around our planet. *Sputnik I* was blasted into space in 1957 and circled Earth for three months. Less than four years later, Soviet cosmonaut Yuri Gagarin became the first person to orbit Earth. Then, in 1969, the world watched with amazement as Neil Armstrong stepped onto the surface of the moon.

Back on Earth, airplanes and flight continued to develop. The Boeing 707, the first large passenger jet, was introduced in the United States in 1954. In 1976 the Concorde SST flew passengers faster than the speed of sound for the first time. The space shuttle *Columbia*, the first piloted spacecraft to make multiple flights, was launched in 1981.

We continue to explore space. In the late 1990s, one cosmonaut spent over a year on the Russian space station *Mir*. And space probes travel far across our solar system to send back data about other planets. Probes have landed on Venus and Mars, while others have photographed Jupiter, Saturn, Uranus and Neptune. The *Cassini* spacecraft, launched in 1997, is one of the largest, heaviest and most complex interplanetary spacecraft ever built. Who knows where space exploration will take people in the future.

The evolution of flight has been unbelievably fast, and look how far it's taken us. It's hard to believe that it all started on a wind-swept dune with just a 12-second flight and the determination and imagination of two brothers, Wilbur and Orville Wright.

The Wright brothers would be delighted to see where their work has taken people.

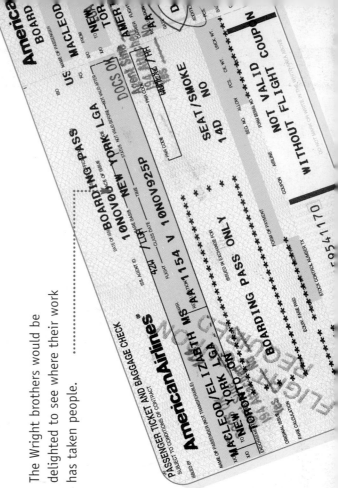

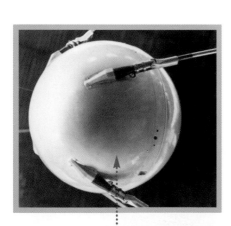

Sputnik I, the first satellite to orbit Earth, was about the size of a basketball.

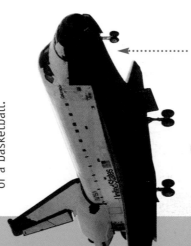

The space shuttle *Columbia* is the first spacecraft that can land at a regular airfield.

At www.jpl.nasa.gov/cassini you can follow the *Cassini* spacecraft's journey to Saturn.

"The Wright brothers created the single greatest cultural force since the invention of writing. The airplane became the first World Wide Web, bringing people, languages, ideas and values together."

— Bill Gates, Microsoft Corporation

The *Apollo 11* astronauts carried cloth from the wing of the Wright brothers' first *Flyer* when they landed on the Moon on July 20, 1969.

Wilbur's and Orville's lives at a glance

1867 April 16 — Wilbur Wright is born in Millville, Indiana

1871 August 19 — Orville Wright is born in Dayton, Ohio

1878 Wilbur and Orville experiment with toy helicopters

1884 The Wright family settles in Dayton, Ohio

1886 Wilbur is hit in the face by a hockey stick and becomes a semi-invalid for almost a year

1889 The Wright brothers' weekly paper, *West Side News*, appears

1892 The Wright brothers open a shop to repair bicycles

mid-1890s Orville and Wilbur first read about Otto Lilienthal, a German engineer who flew in a glider he made himself

1895 The brothers create the Wright Cycle Company to manufacture bicycles

1899 July–August — Wilbur and Orville experiment with a wing-warping kite

1900 The Wright brothers begin testing gliders at Kitty Hawk, North Carolina

1901 July–August — Wilbur and Orville test gliders again at Kill Devil Hills, near Kitty Hawk

Fall — Wilbur and Orville experiment with wind tunnels

1902 The Wright brothers set a time record for glider flight: 26 seconds in the air. They had built the first practical, controllable glider

1903 December 17 — Wilbur and Orville make the world's first controlled, powered flight in the *Flyer*

1904 The brothers build *Flyer II* and continue their flying trials at Huffman Prairie, just outside Dayton, Ohio

1905 Wilbur and Orville build *Flyer III*, the world's first practical airplane

The brothers try to make sales to the U.S., British and French governments

1907 Wilbur and Orville travel to Europe to discuss selling their airplanes

1908 August — Wilbur demonstrates a Wright airplane in France

September 17 — Orville is injured in flying trials put on for the U.S. Army. His passenger, Thomas Selfridge, is killed, the first death in airplane flight

1909 July 30 — The U.S. Army accepts the Military Flyer into service

August — Orville and Wilbur form the German-Wright Company

September–October — Wilbur gives public flying displays in New York

November 22 — The brothers set up the Wright Company in the United States to build airplanes

1910 The Wright brothers begin lawsuits to protect their patents. Their legal battles lasted for years

1911 Orville sets new records in gliding for soaring time

1912 May 30 — Wilbur dies of typhoid fever in Dayton, Ohio

1915 Orville sells the Wright Company. He builds a lab where he continues to experiment

1948 January 30 — Orville dies in Dayton, Ohio, after two heart attacks

The history of flight

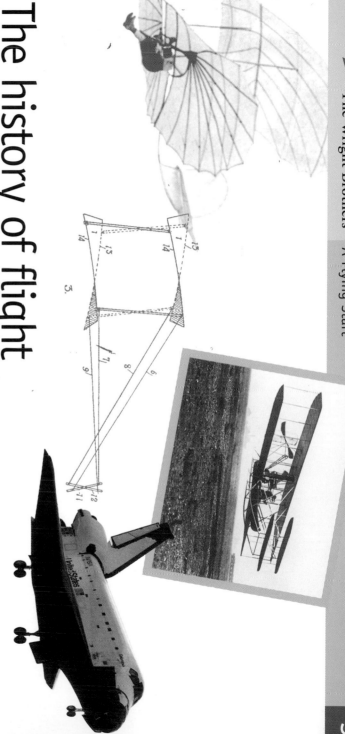

1500 Leonardo da Vinci sketches airplane-like machines

1738 Daniel Bernoulli publishes Bernoulli's principle, which says that as the speed of airflow increases, its pressure decreases

1783 A hot-air balloon created by Joseph and Étienne Montgolfier carries humans aloft for the first time

1854 Sir George Cayley creates a glider that makes a successful take-off

1891–1896 Otto Lilienthal becomes the first to successfully pilot gliders in flight

1903 The Wright brothers make the first controlled, powered flight. Their flying machine flies 36 m (120 ft.) and stays in the air for 12 seconds

1915 The first fighter airplane, *Morane-Saulnier Bullet*, appears

1919 The first flight across the Atlantic Ocean is made by John Alcock and Arthur Whitten Brown. It takes 15 hours and 57 minutes

1927 Charles Lindbergh flies the *Spirit of St. Louis* solo from New York to Paris

1935 The Douglas DC-3 passenger airliner is introduced in the United States

1939 The first successful flight of a jet-engine airplane takes place in Germany

1947 U.S. pilot Chuck Yeager breaks the sound barrier in a rocket-powered aircraft

1954 The Boeing 707, the first large passenger jet, is introduced in the United States

1957 The first human-made satellite, *Sputnik I*, orbits Earth

1961 Soviet cosmonaut Yuri Gagarin is the first person to orbit Earth

1969 U.S. astronaut Neil Armstrong is the first person to set foot on the moon

1976 The first flight of the Concorde SST, the supersonic passenger airplane

1981 The United States launches the space shuttle *Columbia*, the first piloted spacecraft to make multiple flights

1986 Russia's *Mir* space station is launched. It would orbit Earth for more than 15 years

1997 The United States launches the spacecraft *Cassini*. It's expected to reach Saturn in 2004

Visit the Wright brothers

Aviation Trail, Dayton, Ohio

You can tour 47 separate sites in Dayton, Ohio, to find out more about the Wrights and the history of flight. You'll see Huffman Prairie Flying Field, where Wilbur and Orville flew, as well as the original 1905 *Flyer III* (Orville helped restore it), the site of their printing business and more. Try **www.activedayton.com/ partners/cvb/attractions.html** for more information.

The Henry Ford Museum & Greenfield Village, Dearborn, Michigan

Tour the original Wright Cycle Company shop and the house where the Wright brothers lived when they were inventing (both buildings were moved to Dearborn in 1937–38). Look at **www.hfmgv.org** to find out more.

National Air and Space Museum, Smithsonian Institution, Washington, DC

See the world's first airplane (the original 1903 *Flyer*), as well as the 1909 Military Flyer (the world's first military airplane) and other famous airplanes and spacecraft. Surf to **www.nasm.si.edu** to see the Institution's Web site.

Wright Brothers Aeroplane Company & Museum of Pioneer Aviation

Check out **www.wright-brothers.org** to see this virtual museum.

The Wright Brothers National Memorial, Kill Devil Hills, Kitty Hawk, North Carolina

Visit the site of the world's first flight, see the Wright Brothers National Memorial and tour the museum exhibits. Go to **www.nps.gov/wrbr** to take a look at the Web site.

Index